THE GREAT CHALICE OF ANTIOCH

THE
GREAT CHALICE
OF
ANTIOCH

BY

GUSTAVUS A. EISEN

❧

NEW YORK
FAHIM KOUCHAKJI
MCMXXXIII

Copyright 1933
by
Fahim Kouchakji

DESIGNED BY EDWARD B. EDWARDS
PRODUCED BY
ROBERT BLAKE HAMILTON, NEW YORK
AND MADISON SQUARE PRESS

INTRODUCTION

USTAVUS AUGUSTUS EISEN should have been born in the sixteenth or seventeenth century, when universal scholarship was still recognized. Actually he was born on August 2, 1847, in Stockholm, Sweden. Natural history and medieval archaeology were taught by his surroundings, water color and miniature painting were studied under the miniaturist John William Karl Way. As a student at the University of Uppsala, he was friend of the youthful Strindberg, who one morning told him of his miraculous discovery the night before that he was a dramatist. In 1873 he received his degree in science and art and was attached as docent in zoology to the university staff. The young doctor sent to England a presentation copy of his treatise on earthworms, and received in reply a letter saying that by a curious coincidence the writer was also working on earthworms; the letter was signed by Charles Darwin.

Darwin's rival, Agassiz, greatest of science teachers, heard of the young biologist and invited him to America. The invitation was accepted and when Agassiz died shortly after, Doctor Eisen was in California where he was to pass many years as Curator of the California Academy of Sciences.

During these years, his output was enormous. Many of his articles were in his own special field, that of biology, but he found time for excursions into geology, geography, anthropology, and even archaeology. From 1880 to 1903 he was carrying on biological and archaeological surveys in Mexico and Guatemala, collecting material for the Smithsonian Institution and the United States Department of Agriculture.

Nor was his interest confined to pure science. As horticultural editor of the *Fresno Republican* and the *Fresno Expositor,* he popularized the results of scientific enquiries, and later he was editor of *California*. Through his experiments, the quality of grapes was improved, the cultivation of Smyrna figs was made possible, a hardy alligator pear was introduced to the United States. By a vigorous agitation which led to threats on his life by outraged lumbermen, the Sequoia National Park was established in 1890, and the "big trees" of California were saved.

Relics of the Scandinavian past had intrigued his imagination since childhood. With maturity his interests had expanded to take in the puzzle of the Maya pictographs and the strange beliefs of primitive savages. On his retirement from the curatorship of the California Academy of Sciences, he was ready to study the human past through application to archaeology of methods employed in the natural sciences.

Few relics of the past appear more insignificant than beads; to Doctor Eisen they were the fossils which might determine the strata of human history, and he spent years in their study. Glass objects had been treasured by collectors for their beauty; Doctor Eisen traced their history in minute detail. Through this study, as he tells us, he became acquainted with Mr. Fahim Kouchakji, and *The Great Chalice of Antioch* was the result.

As the book slowly made its way to the attention of scholars, heated discussions arose. A few who had not seen the disintegrated silver of the Chalice declared it modern. Many denied its first century date. Doctor Eisen showed himself the true scientist. His work on the Chalice was finished, other work was calling, and he turned to complete his monumental study of antique *Glass* and then to the love of his youth with his recently published *Portraits of Washington*.

Today we realize that in the Chalice of Antioch we have a unique product of the ancient silversmith's art, whose beauty needs no labored description. It is recognized that the portraits of Jesus and of His disciples are the earliest known, and as such must excite the interest of every Christian. The opinion of those most competent to judge now supports, almost without exception, the first century date of the Chalice postulated by Doctor Eisen, and those who yet dissent admit that it is the earliest known example of Christian art.

Doctor Eisen makes no pretense of being an authority on the New Testament, still less is he the historian of the early church. His task to him has been simple, the investigation of an archaeological object. As a working hypothesis, he has assumed that the traditional attribution of the New Testament books is correct and that there is truth in early Christian tradition. The degree to which this hypothesis does actually work may be seen from the following pages.

To those of us who have been trained in the current higher criticism of the New Testament, who have been taught to distrust all traditions of Christian origins not found in the sacred pages, the conclusions of Doctor Eisen are startling, almost uncanny. When the full implication of these conclusions as to the New Testament and early Christian history is realized, there will undoubtedly be more discussion. Meanwhile, at the age of eighty-five, Doctor Eisen with true scientific detachment is content to wait the future test of his conclusions.

A. T. Olmstead.

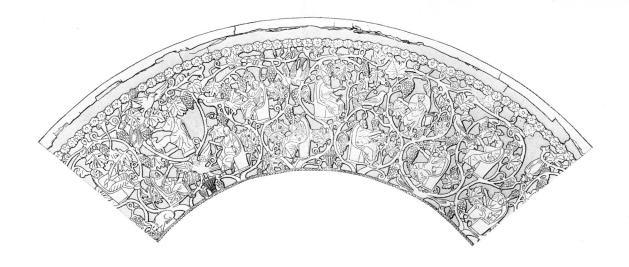

THE GREAT CHALICE OF ANTIOCH

THE Great Chalice of Antioch is named from the Syrian city amid whose ruins it was found. Antioch on the Orontes was founded in 300 B. C. by Seleucus I, the founder of the Seleucid Empire. His son Antiochus I made it the capital of the greatest of the states which followed Alexander the Great. Laid out in symmetrical plan, its straight wide streets paved with Egyptian granite, succeeding rulers adorned it with magnificent palaces, parks, and public buildings, a colonnade four miles long, a temple of Zeus covered with gold plates, a museum to rival that of Alexandria as a center of science.

Pompey put an end to the decaying Seleucid power in 64 B. C., and Antioch became the capital of the Roman province of Syria. Emperor after emperor visited Antioch, enjoyed its charms, and added aqueducts, parks, colonnades and palaces. Antioch was now the largest and most wealthy city of Western Asia. Her baths, games, temples and mansions gave it a deserved reputation for luxury.

Jews had early played an important part in its cosmopolitan life, and it was natural that Christianity should soon find here a foothold. Unknown refugees from Jerusalem made the first converts. Here the followers of Jesus were first called Christians. Here Barnabas and Paul were consecrated for missionary service. Here took place the historic controversy between Peter and Paul. Throughout the Apostolic Period, Antioch remained the headquarters from which missionaries went forth to preach the Gospel (Acts xi, 19; xiii, 1; xv, 22; Galatians ii, 11).

Earthquakes destroyed Antioch during a visit of the Emperor Trajan, but it was rebuilt by Antoninus Pius. Sapor I of the newly revived Persian Empire sacked it horribly (266 A. D.), and it was visited by terrible famines, but always Antioch revived. As Christians became more numerous, the bishop of Antioch gradually assumed the power due his great see. The Roman Empire accepted Christianity under Constantine, who with his mother, Saint Helena, began the construction of a cathedral that was to be of a magnificence appropriate to the great metropolis. Completed by his son Constantius in 341 A. D. its consecration was celebrated by a synod attended by a hundred bishops.

Julian the Apostate visited Antioch in 362 A. D. During the celebration of the mournful pagan rites of Adonis, when torches were carried through the streets, the Vale of Daphne was ravaged by fire and the blame was laid to the Christians. Julian, disgusted with the events, ordered the cathedral to be closed. The cathedral treasurer had hidden the sacred treasures and refused to divulge their hiding place; he died under torture and perhaps they were never recovered.

An earthquake in 526 A. D. is said to have killed a quarter of a million of its inhabitants. Before Antioch could recover from this disaster, it was sacked in 538 A. D. by the Persian Chosroes I so thoroughly that "those who were left could not find the site of their homes." A third time, in 611 A. D., it was sacked by the Persians, this time under Chosroes II. When the Arabs, newly converted to the faith of Mohammed, poured out from the desert, Antioch fell 638 A. D., but was later recovered by the revived Christian empire at Byzantium. The first Crusaders arrived and took Antioch after a year's siege (1098), only to be attacked by the Moslems. They were about to surrender when a Frankish priest was vouchsafed a vision of the Sacred Lance; the spearhead of Longinus was discovered and nerved by its presence, the Crusaders won the victory.

Of the once glorious Antioch, virtually nothing is to be seen above ground. Vanished are the palaces, the temples and baths, and with them the relics of the early Christian disciples. Of the city whose hundreds of thousand inhabitants made it the third largest in the Roman Empire there are today only about thirty thousand residents. A clus-

Christk the Saviour

ter of white buildings at the foot of a steep mountain is all that shows of the site of the famous—and notorious—Grove of Daphne. Forgotten by all but the professional student of ancient history, the Christian natives to this day point out to the visitor the weed grown, rubbish covered hillocks where once the faithful listened to Saint Peter and Saint Paul and where their ancestors worshipped in a magnificent cathedral.

Discovery

One day in 1910, Arab workmen were digging in the ruins of ancient Antioch. Suddenly they came upon a mass of buried silver, in all probability a church treasure hidden in time of danger, whose hiding place had been lost when the man who hid it was dead. Among the objects uncovered was a cross, three book covers, and two chalices, all of silver. They were sold by the original finders to a syndicate of sixteen Arab compatriots who brought them to Aleppo, Syria, and sold them in turn to Kouchakji Frères. From Aleppo they were taken to the Paris gallery of the new owners, where they were skilfully cleaned by the elder André. On the eve of the battle of the Marne, they were removed for safe keeping to New York, where they remain permanently in the possession of Mr. Fahim Kouchakji.

Investigation

Early in April, 1915, Mr. Kouchakji invited me to examine his collection of antique glass, an invitation which ultimately resulted in my book on that subject. In the course of this work, I was shown the treasure from Antioch. The silver book covers, the cross, and the smaller chalice were at once recognized as exceptionally fine examples of early Christian art, which might perhaps date as early as the Fourth Century and were certainly not later than the Sixth. The larger Chalice was obviously far earlier in date and was in fact the most remarkable example of Christian art I had ever seen.

Saint Peter

The following summer was spent in studying the photographs taken before the Chalice was cleaned. By October I had realized that the figures did not give us portrait types but were actual portraits. In April of the next year, I became aware of the significance of the unfinished and mutilated rim of the inner cup. My conclusions as to the character, date, and importance of this unique object were accepted by Professor Josef Strzygowski, the outstanding authority in the field of early Christian art, during a visit in New York, and he wrote the foreword to my monograph, *The Great Chalice of Antioch,* published in 1923.

This monograph is both technical and expensive. Since its publication, a constant stream of letters from all parts of the world has begged me to prepare a more popular account. In response to this justifiable demand, now made more imperative by the public exhibition of the Great Chalice itself at the Century of Progress in Chicago, this brief untechnical account has been prepared.

THE SACRED RELIC

Loosely set in an exquisite open work chalice is the sacred relic, a crude egg shaped cup. The cup is actually unfinished and its only ornamentation, if such it may be

Saint Paul

called, is the rim, turned over outward as a narrow cuff. Good sized pieces have been cut with a sharp tool from its rim, no doubt for the private reliquary of some powerful or eminent Christian of later times such as Constantine or Saint Helena. Except this mutilation, no change has been made in the cup, a relic too sacred for the profanation of any modification whatever. It could hold two and a half quarts of liquid, the capacity to be expected in a Passover Cup, and it is difficult to resist the conviction that at an early date it was connected with the Last Supper.

Saint Jude

THE RELIQUARY

In striking contrast to the crude inner cup is the magnificent reliquary in which it is enshrined. From base of foot to top of rim the Chalice is 7.56 inches high. A narrow circular foot disk with outlines of lotus petals rises to a knob decorated by a wreath, and then a stem. The bowl begins with a corolla of lotus petals arranged in two rows, then comes a plain base band whose upper margin is a bead border. From this border twelve grape vines grow upward and form twelve loops in each of which is posed a seated figure. Between the loops and among the vines are scattered seven doves, an eagle, a butterfly, a lamb, a grasshopper, two snails, two wicker baskets, and a plate with loaves and fish. For the most part, these are held in place by the curved tendrils of the vines. Above the grape vines and just below the turned over rim of the sacred relic is a band of fifty-seven rosettes and a six-pointed star.

Like the sacred cup, the reliquary was made in silver. Frequent handling and kissing of the relic almost obliterated several of the rosettes and began to wear the surface. To preserve it from further injury, the whole Chalice was covered with pale whitish gold leaf. Even this was not enough and still later all but the foot and stem was

Saint James the Lesser

from a horizontal solid disk, often turned on a lathe. Their proportions were not developed free hand, but by a minutely worked out geometric system which determined exactly the outline as well as the height and width of the parts. An example of such chalices may be seen on the Arch of Titus, where we are shown the spoils brought back from the Temple after the capture of Jerusalem in 70 A. D., or in the frescoes of Pompeii, destroyed by Mount Vesuvius in 79 A. D. With the mass production of glass, toward the end of the First Century, when quality gave place to quantity, the geometric system was forgotten, forms were modelled free hand, new types of foot were used to steady the fragile glass. The later type, well illustrated by the smaller chalice of the Antioch treasure, is characterized by a low but wide bowl, a more or less prominent stem, and a wide inverted funnel shaped foot.

THE PORTRAITS

Beautiful and interesting as are the form and details, the portraits excite our deepest interest. The twelve figures fall naturally into two groups, one on either side of the Chalice. In each, the central figure is full face, the others are in profile; four flank the central figure, a fifth is below and to the right. Each figure is seated on a chair within a loop of grape vines and is closely surrounded by branches, leaves, tendrils, and grape clusters, and by various symbols mentioned in the New Testament or known in First Century art. Of the surrounding figures, some are turned right, some left, but all face and hail the central figure with upraised right hand, the ancient salute always given by some nearby individual when the Roman Emperor is depicted in a relief.

All twelve figures possess a quality of portraiture not found in minute sculpture after the First Century. They retain their pleasing qualities and personal characteristics when greatly enlarged, something never found in later works. The closest related portraiture is to be seen in the cameo work of the Augustan period, but even in this period such quality of portraiture as we find on the Chalice is rare.

Each single figure is instinct with life. The effect is largely to be ascribed to a simple procedure which was employed by the majority of Greek artists from early archaic times to the late First Century of the Christian era. By it the subject is represented when the lungs are filled with air. The Greek figures live, mourn, and die in the act of inhalation, and the result is beauty. Lost after the First Century, the method was partially recovered by a few of the Renaissance masters. Our disciples salute the Savior at a moment of inhalation in a gesture full of life, confidence, and exhilaration, a complete contrast to the purely Roman and modern monuments.

Although the poses are similar in all the seated figures, the faces on the Antioch Chalice are so distinct that each has a personality of his own. This is more significant because in all ancient and medieval representations of Christ

gilded a second time with a slightly thicker reddish gold leaf. The two layers of gold leaf have somewhat obscured the more minute details of this exquisite work of the silversmith, but they have preserved the silver which might otherwise have disintegrated during its long centuries of burial in a damp soil. It is significant of the sacred character of the inner cup that it was never desecrated by the gold.

Before or at the time of burial, the silver cup and its container had suffered a blow of such force that both were slightly bent. The blow must have been sustained in ancient times, when the silver was still flexible, for centuries of burial have made it so brittle that we dare not now attempt to restore the original form.

The general scheme, an inner cup with an outer holder, was common enough in the First Century, but in no other instance do we find so exquisite a work of art enshrining so rude an inner cup. The combination of bowl, stem, and foot for chalices and other religious vessels is found from remote antiquity to modern days, but in different periods the relative proportions varied widely.

The Great Chalice of Antioch is identical in type with the known chalices of the first century of the Roman Empire with their ovoid truncated bowls, their very short stems, their low and exceedingly narrow feet, formed and His Disciples hitherto known the portraiture is only diversified by simple variations such as shortening or elongating the beard or hair; we never find such differences in personal, moral, and spiritual characteristics as we should expect in the portrayal of twelve individuals who from the New Testament narratives should be so strikingly different. The complete success of the Chalice artist distinguishes his work from that of all others and proves that these are not merely conventional types but are portraits of living men actually known to the artist, in person or through contemporary portraiture.

Where else is to be seen so glorious an array of early Christian portraiture? Certainly not in the Roman catacomb paintings, on the sarcophagi, or in the illuminated manuscripts, for in all these the faces are moulded on a few types. Leonardo da Vinci in his famous Last Supper painted but four distinct types, on the Chalice we see twelve portraits, no two alike.

Repeatedly the question has been asked: "How do you know whom the figures represent, when their names are not designated in writing? How were their names discovered?"

When the Chalice was first brought to the writer's attention, he was told that the figures of Christ, Peter and John had been tentatively identified. Because of their position, the central figures in front and reverse could only be those of Christ. There should be no surprise that Christ is twice represented on the Chalice, for he is often repeated on the same sarcophagus, where his baptism, his miracles, and other scenes of his life are portrayed side by side. The pose and general appearance of the mature Christ is so similar to the many representations of Christ in later Christian art that there can be no doubt of his identity.

Artists of the early First Century brought as much as they could into a single grouping and everyone knew what was meant. Hercules, Theseus, and other heroes are frequently duplicated on a single object. *An exact parallel to the Youthful and Mature Christ of our Chalice is seen on a cup found in the villa of Boscoreale, which was covered by Mount Vesuvius in 79 A. D. On the anterior face, Augustus is shown as a mature man, on the reverse as a boy; the two figures of Augustus and the two of Christ are all clad in the splendor of the imperial toga.* *See p. 17.*

Thus we have two figures of Christ on the Chalice and accordingly the accompanying figures must be those of his followers. The two groups would then represent Christian scenes, themes, and motifs. All the paraphernalia, emblems, and minor objects on the front face of the Chalice connect directly with the person of Christ as we know him from the New Testament. Our Chalice dates from the First Century and we have therefore every reason to expect actual portraiture. An Egyptian papyrus letter of the next century shows us a common soldier sending his portrait to his father. Life-like portraits in wax technique

Saint Andrew

were painted in the early Second Century at Hawara, an out of the way corner of Egypt. Hellenistic and Early Imperial coins show an astonishingly realistic, sometimes a brutally realistic, portraiture, and are closely related to the art of our Chalice.

The first identification came quite unexpectedly when it was discovered that one of the personages wore about his head a band in the Greek manner and that his face was Greek. This could only be Saint Luke, Evangelist and author of the Acts of the Apostles. He is seated to the right of the Youthful Christ, who displays the New Law, and this suggested that he was placed there in his capacity of Evangelist. This led to the hypothesis that the other three figures in the group were the other three Evangelists. A new discovery added its support. At a much later date, after the first covering of the Chalice with gold foil, the custodian feared that the identity of the personages might be forgotten with the passage of time and of those who originally knew them. He accordingly scratched on the chairs and through the first covering of gold foil certain symbols which would represent each saint. On the chair of Saint Luke he scratched the life symbol, a tree. The chair of Saint Mark has a jug, the water jar of the Last Supper. On Saint Matthew's chair is scratched the arch of the city gate at which he sat and the coin he col-

The Youthful Christ

with thin pliable folds such as would be seen in linen clothing, whereas all the others are dressed in cloaks of heavy folds suggesting woolen materials. The fifth figure in the group could only be Saint Andrew, the brother of Saint Peter and the intermediary who caused John to write the Fourth Gospel.

As will be seen in the sequel, each of the twelve figures possesses certain characteristics or is connected with some symbol which supports the proposed identification. The entire absence of the usual symbols by which the Apostles were later designated proves that these figures were made before the later symbols were invented. Those which are found scratched on the chairs were added much later.

Saint Mark

lected as customs. After this, the identification of the handsome youthful "Beloved Disciple" John and his brother James the Greater naturally followed.

Investigation of the other or anterior group began with Saint Peter, whose identification was sustained by the crossed keys scratched on his chair. In nearly all Christian representations, Saint Peter and Saint Paul face one another, the companion of Saint Peter must be Saint Paul. Their identification is now proved beyond doubt by the portraits of the two Apostles on the somewhat later wall fresco discovered in the underground chapel on the Viale Manzoni in Rome. There the two Apostles are nearly full face, here on the Chalice they are in profile, but the men are undoubtedly the same. That identically the same portraits were painted in Rome and carved at Antioch proves that they were based on authentic representations.

The upper two figures suggested themselves as the two "privileged" Apostles, the two brothers, or cousins, of Christ, Saint James the Lesser and Saint Jude. This identification was confirmed when the author recollected the statement of the Jewish Christian Hegesippus, who lived about the middle of the Second Century, that Saint James was so pious and ascetic that he wore no woolen clothing but only linen. His is the only garment on the Chalice

THE MATURE CHRIST

In the center of the group on the anterior side of the Chalice, more decorative than the reverse, is seated the figure of Christ as a man. His head is rather oblong with rounded dome. The eyes are deep set, the face is refined and decidedly though not conspicuously Semitic, the expression is serene, thoughtful and sympathetic. His hair is short and combed forward in the manner of the First Century. In agreement with the earliest painted representations of Christ, there is no sign of beard.

The posture and mien are dignified and graceful. He is seated on a curule, or camp chair, without back but set upon a conspicuous platform. The feet are bare, probably sandalled, and are drawn back, resting perhaps on a cushion which raised the heels. His costume is a toga over an undergarment, presumably with short sleeves. The drapery end of the upper garment comes down over the left shoulder and reaches below the knees. The other part crosses the chest from the upper right shoulder to the lower right of the chest and across the breast. Further down, it covers the entire right leg to the ankle.

At first, the left forearm and hand were thought to be missing. As shown on the older photographs, they had

Saint John

Saint Matthew

been restored in wax by the elder André, together with three added rosettes, the only restorations ever made on the Chalice and before its unique character was realized. Later it was recognized that the direction of the shoulder proves the arm to be downward. When the Chalice was more thoroughly cleaned in 1931, M. André made a most minute examination and concluded that the arm and hand were concealed under the drapery and that the hand rested on the thigh. He therefore removed the left forearm, added by his father when the Chalice was first cleaned, with the result that the left hand is seen resting on the left

leg above the knee, the remainder of the arm being hidden under the toga. The right hand is extended outward to the right with the palm in the same plane, and almost touches a circular plate which contains seven circular loaves while on the left and upper rim are two fishes.

In the upper row of figures, on a slightly higher level and to the right of Christ, is Saint James, while in a similar position to the left is Saint Jude, his two nearest relatives. In the lower tier of figures, Saint Peter is to the right and to the left Saint Paul. Behind Saint Paul sits Saint Andrew, the elder brother of Peter. All five raise the right hand in salute to the Christ.

Immediately below the platform on which Christ is seated is a Roman eagle with outspread wings, his talons on the loaves in the wicker basket. Directly over the right hand of Christ is the six pointed star, the Star of the Nativity, which like its three nearest rosettes is much worn from the kissing of the sacred relic. Directly above the head of Christ is a horizontally soaring dove, the Holy Spirit. To the right stands a lamb, the "believer," which turns its head backward toward Christ. In the upper row below the third rosette is a helix shell. Below the rosette band above Christ are seen the two most typical lotus buds on long stems.

11

Saint Luke

SAINT PETER

This figure is found to the lower right of Christ, the spectator's left, diagonally downward from the lamb. He is seated, leaning slightly backward in a chair with a high back, his feet resting on the vine stem. With the right arm and hand, he salutes the Christ. The left arm and hand rest on the upper part of the leg.

Saint Peter's head is rounded with cropped curly hair and thick curly beard. The small heavy nose, the small but thick mouth with drooping lip beard, the deeply set eyes present a Jewish type of singular energy and forcefulness. His arms, hands, legs and feet are powerful. The dress is coarse; a woolen tunic covered in places by a cloak whose end is twisted around the right arm. His whole figure is rustic without refinement, a fisherman's body, face and moral strength.

Saint Peter occupies the place of honor with reference to Christ, the right according to the Greek custom and not the left according to Roman. That we actually have here Saint Peter is proved by the identity of the face with the fresco portrait from the underground chapel in Rome, as well as by its similarity to Saint Peter in the Roman catacombs. Further proof may be found in the two crossed keys scratched on his chair by the later guardian.

SAINT PAUL

The figure seated opposite Saint Peter occupies the place second in honor to the left of Christ. Saint Paul is regularly associated with Saint Peter in sculpture, painting, glass, medallions and coins, for from the beginning Saint Paul next after Saint Peter was considered the most important follower of Christ. No representation of Christ with his followers lacks the presence of Saint Paul, who as the principal writer of the Epistles naturally finds his place in this group of the Chalice figures.

Saint Paul is represented as an educated man of great refinement, whose long head and bearded face entirely lack the roughness of Saint Peter. His mien is majestic, his pose judicial and stately. The upper part of his body seems heavier than the lower would warrant, and the legs are decidedly weak. This agrees with the description of Saint Paul's appearance in the Gospel of Paul and Thecla, a work undoubtedly based on accepted tradition. The symbol on the chair is too indistinct to be decipherable, but the exact agreement with the Saint Paul of the Roman chapel fresco makes the identification sure.

SAINT JAMES THE LESSER

Saint James the Lesser was the "brother" of Jesus (Matthew xiii, 55) and the author of an Epistle. These two facts gave him his position on the Chalice, with the writers of the Epistles and in the upper right of the anterior group facing his brother Saint Jude. His figure is of classic design and simplicity, his face refined and of a type above the common laborer. We have already referred to the tradition of Hegesippus, according to which Saint James always wore linen. On the Chalice, his garment falls in thin pliable folds, such as only linen produces, while the dress of all the others shows heavy folds like those produced by wool. The thin texture of the garment permits the outlines of the body to be seen underneath, and gives that apparent elegance of body which is otherwise found only in Saint John.

SAINT JUDE

Opposite Saint James the Lesser is seated his brother Saint Jude to the upper left of Christ. He presents a brotherly resemblance to Saint James and like him has a very handsome face, but a less elastic body. As a writer of a short Epistle, he finds his proper place in a reliquary art. In front of his raised hand is a butterfly with folded wings.

SAINT ANDREW

Outside the group of the four writers of the Epistles is seated Saint Andrew, whose prominence must have dated from his earliest meeting with Christ to whom he brought his younger brother Peter, soon the acknowledged head of the Apostles. He is represented as a very old man, his face full of wrinkles; his body is powerfully built but dignified, rustic but calm and composed. In his left hand he holds a small bag, presumably a purse; it may be that after the treachery of Judas, Peter's brother was for a time in charge of the common funds.

The presence of Saint Andrew on the Chalice in company with the writers of the New Testament is explained by a story in the Muratorian Canon, composed in the Second Century when the memory of the Apostolic period was still fresh. Saint John had in vain been urged by his fellow disciples and bishops to compose a fourth Gospel but had begged them to fast and to inform each other what was revealed to them. That very night in a vision it was revealed to the Apostle Andrew that John should write down everything in his own name and that the others should confirm his account. Their witness is found in John xxi, 24: "This is the disciple which testifieth these things, and wrote these things: and we know that his testimony is true."

THE YOUTHFUL CHRIST

The center of the posterior group is occupied by a figure, seen front view, which without the slightest doubt must represent the Youthful Christ, perhaps at the age of twelve when he taught in the Temple. He is dressed in a toga and seated upon a chair with a high rounded back, the feet resting on a platform in front of the chair. Compared with the portrait of the mature Christ, the difference in age is obvious. The face, since the final cleaning, is full of remarkable detail, thoughtful and most lovable, and expresses preëminently that quality of "soul" discoverable in the work of that master sculptor, the Greek Scopas. His arms are extended. His left hand grasps the two staffs from which the Scroll of the Law descends downward folded on itself. The theme is symbolic, the Youthful Christ extends to the Four Evangelists the New Law, the Gospels they are to write. On the sarcophagi, Christ is often represented in this same pose and we may assume that their theme was inspired by our Chalice.

The four surrounding personages, seated on chairs with high round backs, represent the Four Evangelists, Luke, Mark, John and Matthew. Behind Saint Matthew and Saint John is a fifth personage, Saint James the Greater, the brother of Saint John, in strict parallel to the fifth personage in the anterior group, who is Saint Andrew, brother of Saint Peter. The two symbolic representations in this group are the Scroll of the Law held by the Youthful Christ and the fruits of the Tree of Life appropriately assigned to Saint Luke the Physician. Two large doves seated on a vine branch face Christ on either side and seem to be included in the general series of animals, the believers in Christ.

SAINT LUKE

In the place of honor to the right of the Youthful Christ is Saint Luke. Around his head and passing over his forehead is the fillet band, in common use by the Greeks, but

Saint James the Greater

not by true Orientals. His face, without trace of Jewish features, is characteristically Greek, such a type as we find on the Hellenistic stela of the physician Jason and that of the physician-god Asclepias from the healing shrine at Epidaurus. The three balls before him are the fruits of the Tree of Life, from early times the symbol of a physician. In later Christian symbolism, they correspond to the three hosts of the Eucharist. Their connection with the Evangelist is proven by the early Christian relief where an angel offers Saint Luke a plate with the three fruits of the Tree of Life. The Tree itself seems to be scratched on his chair.

SAINT MARK

Without doubt the most remarkable portrait on the Chalice is that which occupies the second place of honor, to the lower right of the Youthful Christ. According to the History of the Patriarchs of Alexandria, Saint Mark was born west of Egypt in the Cyrenaica. His once wealthy parents lost their money and emigrated to Syria where Saint Mark spent his youth as a water carrier. From other sources we learn that he was in some manner deformed and that he carried water both to the Feast at Cana and to the Last Supper. Christ is believed to have referred to him as the "man bearing a pitcher of water" who was to lead the two disciples to the guest chamber where the Passover was to be eaten (Mark xiv, 13; Luke xxii, 10). This identification was accepted by the early guardian of the Chalice who scratched the water jug on his chair. His heavy manual labor made him a useful body helper to Saint Paul and Saint Barnabas on their missionary travels (Acts xii, 25).

The portrait of Saint Mark on the Chalice is exactly what we should expect from this account. The beauty and elasticity of the eleven other figures are completely lacking. Instead, we have the enormously developed shoulders, the heavy arms and huge hands, the short sunken neck, the bent back, the splay feet of a man who in his youth carried on his shoulders an immense water jar. His head is forced permanently upward by his heavy burden, his eyes stare up and out, the funnel shaped corner of his mouth indicates that like other oriental water carriers he strengthened the call of his wares by forcing out his voice through the corner of his mouth. So pathetically homely is his face that only the truth of actual portraiture could have won it a place on this beautiful work of art.

SAINT MATTHEW

Seated opposite Saint Mark is a sedate, dignified and business like person who can only be Saint Matthew. The high head, the small mouth, the prominent forehead, the practical mien, all suggest the shrewd administrator who sat at the arched gate the guardian has scratched on his chair, and collected the coin he has also represented from those who brought their wares into the city until Christ called him from his work to be his Apostle. Although a publican, he remained a pious Jew for his right forearm is wound with the only example of a phylactery known from this period.

SAINT JOHN

A youthful man is seated in the upper left of the second group. His body is slender and elastic; his features are handsome and the proportions of the body graceful. His face, though injured by time, is remarkably sweet and thoughtful, contemplative and full of mystery and sadness. Such features illustrate perfectly the traditions connected with the Apostle John, while his presence with the other Evangelists on the Chalice proves conclusively that he and not the Disciple John was the author of the Fourth Gospel.

The characteristic head, with its almost spherical outline, indicates a close connection with the next figure and suggests that they were related. There were three sets of brothers among the Apostles, Peter and Andrew, the sons of Jona, James and Jude, the sons of Alphaeus or Clopas, and John and James, the sons of Zebedee. Since the others are already accounted for, these two brothers must be John and James. These brothers bore the epithet "Sons of Thunder," but neither on the Chalice nor in any other

representation does Saint John deserve the appellation. Here he is rather the personification of that gentleness we expect from what we learn of him in the Scriptures.

SAINT JAMES THE GREATER

Behind Saint Matthew and just outside the second group is the most youthful figure of the Disciples. The spherical formation of the head denotes a relationship with Saint John, the only other man on the Chalice with a head of that shape. He must accordingly be Saint John's brother, Saint James the Greater. He was older than Saint John but was put to death by Herod Agrippa I in 44 A. D. (Acts xii, 2). Thus when at a later date the Chalice portraits were carved there could be no portraits of him as an older man and the artist had no other choice than to represent him as he appeared toward the end of his short life.

Saint James and his brother were called "Sons of Thunder." This is the only face on the Chalice which in its enthusiasm and self consciousness does justice to such an appellation. His lips actually demand: "Master, we would that thou shouldest do for us whatsoever we shall desire," and "Grant unto us that we may sit, one at thy right hand and the other on thy left hand, in thy glory" (Mark x, 35, 37). He seems quite capable of asking: "Lord, wilt thou that we command fire to come down from heaven and consume them, even as Elias did?" (Luke ix, 54).

DECORATIVE UNITS

After the portraits, the *decorative units* come next in importance. Bands of rosettes were in common use during the First Century before and after Christ. Many of the early Samian and Arretine pottery cups are decorated in this fashion, for example the cup signed by Tigranes in the Metropolitan Museum of Art. The star above the hand of Christ is the only star in which the early Christians could have been interested, the *Star of Bethlehem*.

The grape vines, twelve in number, render the whole aspect strong and harmonious. They cover all space not devoted to other decoration, yet without the slightest impression of crowding, and they form the twelve loops for the seated figures. The vines are in full growth, with leaves and end buds, sometimes in the form of the lotus, and also a few flowers which are setting berries. Vines of like form and manner of branching are seen on various altars and table stands excavated in Pompeii, and are painted in the Catacomb of Domitilla at Rome which dates about 90 A. D. The larger grape leaves are similar to those on the puteals or well curbs of Pompeii, where the stem of each vine crosses the other on the side of the puteal while on the front face the top branches meet by turning inwards.

The grape tendrils are bold, heavy, well defined, and often conspicuously forked as are those of the Naples

Cameo Vase whose First Century date cannot be disputed. *Vine binding* in the upper horizontal branches is accomplished either by tendrils or by strings joining the branches two and two, where they overlap directly above the six figures in the upper row of loops. Not less than fifty-four such different tendril bindings, none later than Trajan, are found on the early red glazed pottery. *Lotus buds* on long threadlike stems with two or three petals, the two outer in relief, the center one seen full face, are found on the Chalice. They are known only in the Augustan period and never occur on objects later than the First Century.

The eagle and the *basket of loaves* below the feet of Christ symbolize the Roman Empire partaking of the blessings of Christianity through its Eucharist as administered by Saint Peter and Saint Paul. Similar *Eucharistic baskets* are represented in the Roman Catacombs. The representation is entirely justified, since until the Christians were accused of the burning of Rome they were not persecuted but were tolerated and even protected.

The doves, except for the one directly above the head of Christ which stands for the Holy Spirit, have no special relation to the personages in their vicinity and may be considered as simply decorative. However, symbolism is possible (Matthew x, 16), for dove amulets in the round were used by both Christians and pagans, and near many doves in the Catacomb paintings stand the words: "Innocent and simple souls." On a well curb from Pompeii, the doves in downward flight resemble those on the Chalice.

The rabbit is found on the ground line between two loops, in a crouching position and nibbling on a cluster of grapes. Eyes, hair, and the like are modelled naturally and in detail. Similar naturalistic rabbits are common in First Century art. *The lamb* which turns its head to the central figure is the *believer in Christ,* who turns to him for physical, bodily and spiritual protection.

Date of the Great Chalice of Antioch

The date of the Chalice is established, not by conjecture, but by the known dates of each of its elements, form, proportion, and decoration. *The form of the Chalice is paralleled by eleven silver cups of chalice form found in the villa of Boscoreale which was destroyed by Mount Vesuvius in 79 A.D.,* by cups and wall paintings from Pompeii, destroyed in the same eruption, by a glass chalice and other cups which cannot be dated later than the First Century. A foot similar to that of the Chalice was used even before the First Century but the chalices manufactured later than that date had an inverted funnel shaped foot, not the flat solid or slightly concave foot rings of the early type.

Human figures superimposed in the manner of the Chalice and seated in chairs are also found on the red glazed pottery and on the vases from Maara in Syria which date from the First Century. The chairs with high rounded backs cannot however be employed to date the Chalice, as they were used in late Minoan times, were common with the Greek figurines from Tanagra, and continued in the Roman Catacomb representations.

Animals on the base line were common both on reliefs and on paintings of vases in the First Century. *The front face of the Chalice is practically repeated on the Naples Cameo Vase, where the vines have the same form and the Antique Mask occupies exactly the same position as the Eagle on the Chalice, while the Christ of the Chalice is replaced by a rectangle with rosettes. See p. 17.*

Rosette bands are found on innumerable red glazed ware vases in the same position as on the Chalice and all datable to the First Century. Specimens of such ware are in almost every museum of Europe and America. We find the same bands on the Maara Syrian vases, on the Seven Branched Candlestick from the Jerusalem Temple, represented on the Arch of Titus, on the silver vessels from Boscoreale and Hildesheim, all with certainty of the First Century.

Zigzagged vine stems are found on the Naples Cameo Vase, where their knee junctions are covered in the manner of the Chalice, in the Domitilla Catacomb of 90 A.D., and on Pompeiian table stands. The forked vine tendrils are not found later than the Emperor Hadrian, but were common before that time, the lotus buds are found on vines only before the early Second Century.

From the dates of these details we must conclude that the Chalice was made in the last third of the First Century. Details such as those we have mentioned are not found in connection with objects later than the earliest part of the Second Century, and in general not later than the last half of the First.

Sacred Vessels

Relics and amulets which have come down to us from early Christian times make known to us many symbols. Some are emblematic, for instance, fish stood for Christ and loaves for spiritual food. Simple dots represent the drops of blood. Other objects illustrate their originals, such as the broken spear that pierced Christ's side or the round platter for the paten. Only a small number have the form of vessels; semi-circular cups with low foot stand and very narrow base, beakers, pitchers, narrow pointed cones, amulets shaped like bambinos with large flat tops and with crossed bands like spiral body wrappings. All stood for some incident or object of the Christian faith. The most sacred relics must have been those connected with Christ, by possession, use, or association, and especially those of his passion. Of these relics we possess copies, some fantastic and without even approximate likeness, others depicted with such precision as to inspire our confidence. The vessels connected with Christ are not many, all mentioned in the Scripture or in early Christian tradition. We know the following:

The Water and Wine Jars of Cana, nearly always illustrated as the typical wine vessel, the amphora, more rarely as water vessels without handles.

The Dish of the Paschal Lamb, always a flattish plate able to stand alone and large enough to hold a supper for twelve.

The Water Jug carried to the Last Supper by Saint Mark is frequently illustrated as on his chair on our Chalice, a medium sized water jug with one handle.

The Cup of Gethsemane was not a material vessel and must have vanished with the angel. It is rarely represented and always at a late date.

The Vessel of Joseph of Arimathea in which he collected the Blood of Christ is represented as a cylindrical beaker, wide at the top, and always decorated with a bent or broken spear. It is often found in minute amulets and always surrounded by an openwork holder.

The Jug of Joseph of Arimathea in which he carried the sacred blood has always the form of a cruet and could not have been an open vase.

The Cup of the Eucharist varies in form in the various copies. As a rule, the bowl is large, the foot and stand small. On represented Eucharistic tables we find both cylindrical beakers and lower chalice cups, for the earlier Christians seem to have used no special form. When it is shown on tombstones as the Cup of Life, it generally has the form of our Chalice, a possible reminiscence of the original cup used by Christ in instituting that sacrament.

During the excavation of Gezer in Palestine, there was unearthed a Fourth Century lamp with a representation of a cup similar to the Chalice and flanked by two sacred doves. It is evident that the potter wished to portray the Cup of Life, the Eucharist, and it is clear that he or a predecessor must have seen our Chalice to reproduce its proportions so correctly.

Traditions of the Cup of the Last Supper continued in Jerusalem after the Crucifixion. They are mentioned in our canonical Gospels and in the Gospel of Nicodemus. Joseph of Arimathea is stated to have had the Cup of the Last Supper in his possession. A more elaborate account is found in the *"Treasure Cave"* literature which sprang up about the middle of the Fourth Century. During this period, cups purporting to be that of the Last Supper were continuously on display in Jerusalem. One of these cups in the Cathedral of Saint John was touched by pilgrims through an opening in its reliquary.

THE GRAIL

Medieval Grail romances, generally called *Legends of the Holy Grail,* flourished in the Twelfth Century. They were based on older writings, which can be traced back to the Orient, and even the contemporary additions are again for the most part from oriental sources. They divide naturally into two series.

One, the *Early History,* is localized at Jerusalem and in Palestine south and into Egypt. It describes how Joseph of Arimathea came into possession of the Cup of the Last Supper, how he was forced to leave the country, how he found protection at the court of a pagan king who was soon converted, and how he left for the "West," which may here mean Crete or Cappadocia. Without doubt it was composed by Coptic monks who were well acquainted with their native Egypt. Names of localities and individuals are usually Egyptian, but the saints mentioned are Persian.

The second series is known as the *Quest of the Holy Grail.* We are told how Joseph of Arimathea went to England, only to find that the Grail had arrived before him and dwelt in its Castle Corbenic, in Syriac the "House of the Eucharist," how the Grail came and went of its own accord, how the three questers, Gawan, Percival, and Galahad each sought to find the Grail, and how it was finally brought back to Syria, to Heaven, or to some unmentioned place, according to the particular manuscript version we accept.

Even in this section, the general story and many of the details are of Oriental origin. Galahad is Syrian, or rather Biblical, Gawan is Persian, and now it is reported that even Wolfram's *Parzival* is derived from two decidedly early Persian poems, one the *Pearl Song,* the other the *Story of Parsiwal,* which would exclude a Celtic origin for the Parzival Quest. The Persian poem must have been brought back to Europe by the Crusaders and in various translations utilized by Provencal, German and British troubadours and poets for their *Quests of the Holy Grail.* The story of Joseph of Arimathea and the Cup of Christ is found in various so-called *Gospels* of the early church and was accepted by the Christians of the first four centuries.

Those who believe that the inner cup of the Great Chalice of Antioch might have been preserved as a sacred relic because it was actually used by Christ and his Apostles at the Last Supper have called it the Holy Grail. Such a term can be applied only to the inner cup, for the Chalice holder is of somewhat later date and was made only as a reliquary to enshrine the precious relic. That Chalice, as we have abundantly proved, cannot be later than the First Century. Thus at a time when many who had known Christ in the flesh were still living, the inner cup was enshrined as the noblest Christian relic. The only cup which explains such reverence would be that by which Christ instituted the Eucharist.

Naples Vase and Antioch Chalice

Three corresponding views of the principal details of the Antioch Chalice sides and the Naples Vase. In center, the Naples Vase, with certainty of the First Century, showing the similarity in pose and design, and consequently the date of the sculptures.

The Augustus Cup

Two views, front and reverse, of the silver cup of Augustus first Roman Emperor, 29 B.C.–14 A.D., now in the Rothschild Collection, Paris. Found at Boscoreale, near Pompeii. Shows two views of the seated Emperor, youthful and mature. The similarity in pose and design of these portrait figures to the two Christ figures on the Antioch Chalice furnishes one of the most conspicuous proofs of the Chalice date.

Saint James the Lesser

Christ the Saviour

Saint Jude

Saint Peter

Saint Paul

Saint Andrew

CHRIST, APOSTLES AND EVANGELISTS. Original Etchings on Copper, after the sculptured portraits on the Antioch Chalice, by the distinguished artist Margaret West Kinney.

Upper. SAINT JAMES THE LESSER seated to the upper right of Christ. His is a noble face and ascetic. He was called the "brother" of the Lord and was also the first Bishop of Jerusalem. One of the most distinguished portraits on the Chalice.

Lower. SAINT PETER occupies the place of honor to the right of Christ. The strong face and dominating mien of this portrait are characteristic of the mind and accomplishments of this great Apostle.

Upper. The sublime face of CHRIST THE SAVIOUR, a mature man, but young, looks forth from the center front of the Chalice, beardless and with his hair combed forward in the fashion of the First Century. His face is definitely but not emphatically Semitic. His expression is serene and spiritual. He is here the Saviour, the redeemer of mankind.

Lower. SAINT PAUL is shown in the second place of honor to the left of Christ. His is a gentle, lovable face and his fine, upright and dignified pose are in full agreement with what we know of him as the intrepid Apostle. This is the earliest portrait of St. Paul known and unlike all others, with the exception of that in the fresco in Via Manzoni, the only one which contains actual and convincing personal characteristics.

Upper. SAINT JUDE is seated to the upper left of Christ. He was one of the two nearest earthly relatives of Jesus and a "privileged" Apostle. His face is refined and sincere in expression, indicating a noble character. He must have been a very handsome man. On the Chalice sculpture one sees before him a butterfly with folded wings. An almost perfectly preserved miniature sculpture.

Lower. SAINT ANDREW is placed just behind Saint Paul in the lower row of figures. He is portrayed as a very old man and his astonished expression recalls the tradition that the Holy Spirit communicated through him the command that John compose the Fourth Gospel.

Saint Luke

The Youthful Christ

Saint John

Saint Mark

Saint Matthew

Saint James the Greater

Upper. SAINT LUKE is seated to the upper right of the youthful Christ. The Greek headband and the Grecian head and face are sustaining proofs of his identity. The refinement and intellect in his portrait really indicate "a man of great kindness and a skillful physician," as this beloved companion of Paul is known to have been.

Lower. ST. MARK is seated to the right of the youthful Christ in the place of honor, corresponding to that of Saint Peter on the front of the Chalice; one the founder of the Coptic Church, and the other the founder of the Church of Rome. His face is remarkable for its strength and uncouth features, and indicates enormous energy and purpose.

Upper. THE YOUTHFUL CHRIST, as a boy of about twelve, is portrayed in the center of the second Chalice group. The beautiful face is in the style of the school of the sculptor Scopas, indicating that the artist had studied the works of this Greek master. Christ is here symbolically displaying the scroll of the New Law to the four Evangelists seated around him. The photograph on a previous page shows the almost perfect preservation of the sculpture, which stands out in unsurpassed sweetness and beauty.
Lower. SAINT MATTHEW, to the left of the youthful Christ, has a fine head. The small upper lip and the contented expression of the face are features which impress the viewer, and convince one that this must be a faithful portrait of a man who always placed duty first.

Upper. SAINT JOHN is seated to the upper left of the young Christ. The mystic, beardless face, the energetic action, are worthy of detailed study· The outline of the head shows resemblance to that of his brother, Saint James the Greater. They possess much family likeness but, also, decided differences. In St. John, goodness seems prevailing; in St. James, alertness and activity.

Lower. SAINT JAMES THE GREATER is seated just behind Saint Matthew. The smooth youthful face, without beard, indicates that he was a young man when his portrait was taken. Saint James was first of the Apostles to die and therefore never attained great age. He was forceful and enthusiastic and here seems actually speaking.

NOT of such early date nor such elegance and style, but extremely interesting and fine in their period are five Christian silver objects found at the same time and place as the Great Chalice of Antioch. All are of a religious nature and vastly important as they show that the Chalice was not a solitary, accidental object, but part of a cherished collection of sacred belongings of an early, wealthy Christian Basilica. They, too, have suffered from centuries of burial so that the silver is crystalized, reflecting the sheen only in places.

THE BOOK COVERS OF SILVER

These repoussé silver book covers belonged to three different manuscript codices and were originally affixed to wooden covers of now unknown works, presumably Gospels or Epistles. The silver has become crystalized and brittle by time and contact with the soil.

The date is established by four small vases in the corners of the cover showing the cross supported by two saints. These "mystic" vases are best dated to the Fifth Century. Vases like these containing holy oils or ointments were used in Christian rites. The practice of representing Christ, Apostles and Saints under arches supported by columns began centuries before; but the columns on two of these covers are like those from the Temple in Jerusalem, now in the Basilica of St. Peter's in Rome. The use of holy figures both indicated the contents and served as amulets. Thus Saint Paul would be suitable for the cover to a book of his Epistles. The Holy Cross supported by angels would protect the whole New Testament, and Saint John, with the ceremonial cross, would indicate the Codex with his Gospel and the Apocalypse.

Cover with a Saint Holding a Cross. The Saint may be Saint John as Bishop of Jerusalem, standing under an arch of palm leaves and between twisted columns. The decorations include two peacocks, corner trefoils, baskets with loaves of bread, lanterns, vine leaves and a mystic vase at the lower center from which the vines develop.

Cover with Two Saints and a Large Cross. Two Saints uphold an enormous cross. The central arm supports two bound Gospels with decorative covers. In the corners are four mystic vases from which vines issue and untwine. In the circular spaces are grape clusters, grape leaves, ivy leaves, the evergreen being symbolic of life, and a loaf, a basket and birds.

Cover with a Saint Holding a Gospel. This may be Saint Paul, judging from his facial characteristics. In its simplicity the figure is remarkably imposing and dignified. He holds in his hands a bound Gospel. Otherwise the decorations are similar to the one with Saint John holding the cross.

THE LESSER CHALICE

This chalice is known as the "Lesser" to distinguish it from the Great Chalice of Antioch with which it was found. It belongs to the type of "literati" or inscribed chalices of a form characteristic of early Medieval times. The wide spherical bowl is slightly wider at the girdle than at the rim, while the inverted funnel-shaped foot recalls the practical stands from the beginning of the Fourth Century. On the bowl and continued on the foot in precise and well executed Greek lettering, is this inscription: "For repose of Charouphas and salvation of Thecla and their children." Inside the foot is the maker's name.

The inscription seems to be the only decoration of the chalice and is bordered with rows of tooled lines, the upper giving the effect of rope. It was covered inside and out, originally, with gold leaf and was no doubt a communion cup in the Basilica. The general characteristics are that the bowl is large as compared to its height, the footstand is low and well proportioned and the whole composition is pleasing. A few chalices of similar appearance have been found in Syria.

THE CROSS

This belongs to the class of ceremonial crosses carried in religious processions and used in holy rites. It is 105 cm. from top to bottom and 95 cm. across the arms. There is no evidence that it was used as a crucifix, for any additional covering would have hidden the Greek inscriptions which extend from top to bottom and across the arms, on both faces. The silver covering of the central square where the arms meet is missing. This silver was in two sheets which were nailed from front to back and from back to front over an original wood cross.

Of the silver nails used, 108 are still in position, although the old wood has decayed and has been restored. Considering its size and age, the cross, although fragile, can be considered as in good condition. This cross is similar in type to that seen in the hands of a saint on one of the book-covers. The incomplete Greek inscription has not yet been successfully deciphered.

Upper Row. Three Large Silver Book Covers, also of the find. Fifth Century. They are made in repoussé technic and were evidently the upper covers for three early codices. The mystic vases in the corners of one of the covers indicate the date, as these were most typical of that period. A cross similar to the one in the hands of the saint is found on an ivory plaque in the Stroganow collection. *Height 27 cm.*

Center. Silver Ceremonial Cross, with Greek Inscriptions. Fifth Century. Part of the Great Chalice of Antioch Find. *Height 105 cm. Width 95 cm.*

Lower Center. Silver Communion Cup with two bands of Greek Letters, and with Bowl and Funnel Shaped Foot. Fifth Century. Known as the Lesser Chalice. *Height 19 cm. Diameter 17.5 cm.*

21

BIBLIOGRAPHY

Annual of the American Schools of Oriental Research, V. 1925.

BACON, B. W. Eagle and Basket on the Antioch Chalice. (Annual of the American Schools of Oriental Research, V. 1925.)

BARTON, GEORGE A. Archaeology and the Bible. American Sunday School Union, Philadelphia, pp. 514-518, 1 pl.

BEAUPLAN, ROBERT DE. La Plus Ancienne Image du Christ. Une Représentation Iconographique de Jésus datant du Premier Siècle de Notre Ere. (*L'Illustration*, June 7, 1924.)

BREHIER, LOUIS. Les Trésors d'Argenterie Syrienne et L'Ecole Artistique d'Antioche. (*Gazette des Beaux-Arts*, 1920.)

BURKITT, F. C. The Chalice of Antioch. (*Cambridge Review*, Feb. 29, 1924, p. 253.)

CABROL, F. *Dictionnaire d'Archéologie Chrétienne et de Liturgie.* Fsc. LXVII, LXIX. 1925.

COBERN, CAMDEN M. New Archaeological Discoveries and their Bearing upon the New Testament. Funk & Wagnalls Co., pp. 550-552.

CONROW, WILFORD S. Accent of the Figures. (*The Great Chalice of Antioch*, by G. A. Eisen. pp. 87-93.)

COOK, ARTHUR BERNARD. The Chalice of Antioch. (*The Cambridge Review.* XLV. pp. 213-216. Feb. 15, 1924.)

————The True Portraits of the Authors of the Gospels and the Four Evangelists on the Chalice of Antioch. (*London Illustrated News.* June 7, June 14, June 21, 1924.)

————The Chalice of Antioch. (*London Illustrated News.* Aug. 1924.)

————A Study of Ancient Religion. Zeus. Vol. II, part II, pp. 1197-1210. (Cambridge University Press.)

DALTON, O. M. *East Christian Art.* A Survey of the Monuments. (Oxford, 1925.)

DIEHL, CHARLES. L' Ecole Artistique d'Antioche et les Trésors d'Argenterie Syrienne. (*Syria.* II. 1921. pp. 81-95. Pl. IX-XIV.)

————Preface to *Catalogue d'Exposition d'Art Byzantin*, Louvre, Paris, 1931.

————Manuel d'Art Byzantin. 2nd ed. Tome T. Paris, 1925.

DUNNEY, REV. JOSEPH A. The Mass. Macmillan Co., 1925.

DUSSAUD, RENÉ. Les Monuments Syriens a l'Exposition d'Art Byzantin. (*Syria.* Tome XII, 1931.)

Earliest, The . . Chalice. The Antioch Chalice. (*London Times*, Jan. 17, 1924. pp. 12, 15, 16.)

EDWARDS, EDWARD B. Diagrams for Dynamic Analysis of the Chalice, (*The Great Chalice of Antioch* by G. A. Eisen, pp. 184.)

EISEN, GUSTAVUS A. Preliminary Report on the Great Chalice of Antioch. Earliest Portraits of Christ and the Apostles. (*Amer. Jour. of Arch.*, II Ser., XX, 1916. pp. 426-437. pl. XIX. figs. 1-4.)

————The Plate with the Seven Loaves and Two Fishes. (*Amer. Jour. of Arch.* II Ser., Vol. XXI, 1917. pp. 77-79.)

————The Date of the Great Chalice of Antioch. (*Amer. Jour. of Arch.* II Ser., Vol. XXI, 1917. pp. 169-186.)

————Portraits of Christ, Apostles and Evangelists: Identification of the Seated Figures. (*New Era Magazine*, Jan. 1920, pp. 12-45. 4 figs. June, 1920. pp. 414-417; July, 1920. pp. 526-528. 6 figs.)

————Do Portraits Exist of Peter and Paul? Comparison of Pictures in Catacombs with Sculptures on Chalice of Antioch. (*International Studio.* LXXVII, June, 1923. pp. 215-220. 8 figs.)

————*The Great Chalice of Antioch:* Earliest Portraits of Christ, Apostles and Evangelists. 2 Vol. in-folio, New York, 1923. Kouchakji Frères. Vol. I, Text and Diagrams; Vol. II, Photogravures after Original negatives by Author and Fahim Kouchakji. Reproduced by A. W. Elson. Detail Drawing by Lindsley F. Hall. Twelve original etchings on copper by Margaret West Kinney. Foreword by Josef Strzygowski.

————The Great Chalice of Antioch. (*Biblical Review*, XI, 1926. pp. 40-75.)

Encyclopedia Universal ilustrada Europeo-Americana. T. XXVIII, 2ª p. 2709, 1926.

HUSSLEIN, REV. JOSEPH (S. J.). An Ancient Mass-Relic. (*America*, Apr. 5, 1924, pp. 588-589.) Mass Symbols on the Antioch Chalice. (*America*, May 10, 1924.)

————The Holy Grail in New York? (*Columbia*, Mar. 1925, pp. 9, 10, 11, 32.) What Did Christ Look Like? (*Columbia*, Apr. 1925, pp. 9, 10, 11, 45.) As Men Saw the Apostles. (*Columbia*, June, 1925, pp. 18, 19, 42.)

JACKSON, REV. F. J. FOAKES. The Antioch Chalice. Its Discovery and Age. (*The Churchman*, Feb. 2, 1929; Feb. 9, 1924.)

————The Chalice of Antioch. The Individual Figures. (*The Churchman*, Aug. 16, 1924.) As Between Experts. (*The Churchman*, Aug. 23, 1923.)

JERPHANION, G. DE (S. J.). Le Calice d'Antioch a l'Exposition d'Art Byzantin, *Byzantion*, T. VI, fasc. II. 1931. Bruxelles.

Journal of Roman Studies. XIV, 1924. London. pp. 281-286.

KAUFMAN, CARL MARIA. *Handbuch der Christlichen Archäologie*, 3rd ed. Paderborn, 1922. pp. 541-544. Fig. 271.

KINNEY, MRS. M. W. Diagrams of the Occulted Spirals in the portraits (*The Great Chalice of Antioch* by G. A. Eisen. pp. 185.)

LANIER, HENRY WYSHAM. (*American Review of Reviews*, Dec. 1924. pp. 634-639.)

LEBRUN, HECTOR. Le Calice d'Antioch. (*La Jeunesse*, Dec. 9, 16, 1920.) 16, 1920.)

McDANIEL, W. B. The Great Chalice of Antioch. (*Classical Weekly*, XVIII, 1925, pp. 123-127.)

MAYNARD, REV. JOHN A. The Great Chalice of Antioch. (*The Living Church*, LXXII. Feb. 28, 1925. pp. 595-597. 2 fig.)

MONTGOMERY, JAMES A. A Note on the Great Chalice of Antioch. (*Amer. Jour. of Arch.* II Ser., Vol. XXI, 1917. pp. 80-81.)

NEWBOLD, WM. ROMAINE. The Great Chalice of Antioch. (*The Ladies Home Journal*, Nov., 1924.)

————The Eagle and the Basket on the Great Chalice of Antioch. (*Amer. Jour. of Arch.* II Ser., Vol. XXIX, 1925.)

PIJOAN. *History of Art.* Vol. 2. Pl. VI. Harper Bros., N. Y. 1929.)

SMOTHERS, REV. R. EDGAR. The Chalice of Antioch. (*Fortnightly Review.* Mar., 1925. pp. 98-99.)

STRZYGOWSKI, JOSEF. Der Silberkelch von Antiochia. (*Jahrbuch der Asiatischen Kunst.* 1925. pp. 53-61. Pl. 122.)

————Foreword (*The Great Chalice of Antioch* by G. A. Eisen, Vol. I.)

For a full bibliography see Eisen: *The Great Chalice of Antioch.* Compare also Library Indexes for Articles in periodicals and newspapers.